PREFACE

The study of accountancy is a cornerstone of the business and finance sectors, serving as a critical tool for financial management, decision-making, and organizational growth. The course IGNOU BCA Accountancy 1 Previous Year Unsolved Papers ECO 2, offered by the Indira Gandhi National Open University (IGNOU), is a crucial component for students pursuing a degree in commerce or related fields. The rigorous curriculum of this course demands that students not only grasp the fundamental principles of accounting but also apply this knowledge to practical financial problems. To aid students in their pursuit of excellence in this subject, this book presents a comprehensive collection of previous years' unsolved papers of the ECO-02 course.The rationale behind compiling these unsolved papers is to provide students with a valuable resource that enhances their understanding of accountancy and prepares them effectively for examinations. These papers serve as a vital tool for self-assessment, allowing students to evaluate their knowledge, pinpoint areas needing further study, and practice solving problems within the time constraints typically encountered in exams. Moreover, engaging with these papers will help students develop the analytical thinking and problem-solving skills essential for success in the accounting profession.

This book is meticulously organized to meet the needs of students at various levels of expertise. Each paper included in this compilation has been carefully selected from different years to cover a wide range of topics within the ECO-02 syllabus. The problems presented range from fundamental accounting tasks to more complex scenarios that test a student's ability to prepare, analyze, and interpret financial statements. By attempting these unsolved papers, students will not only reinforce their theoretical knowledge but also gain practical experience in addressing real-world accounting challenges.In addition to serving as an academic resource, this book is also intended to instill confidence in students as they prepare for their examinations. The exposure to diverse problems will familiarize students with the types of questions that are likely to appear in exams, enabling them to approach their studies with a strategic mindset. This book encourages a deeper exploration of the subject, prompting students to engage with the material beyond the standard textbook content and to think critically about accounting practices.

We extend our heartfelt thanks to the students and educators who have contributed to the creation of this book. Their insights and feedback have been instrumental in ensuring that this compilation meets the highest standards of academic excellence. As you embark on your journey through the field of accountancy, we hope that this book will serve as a dependable companion in your studies, helping you to unlock your full potential in the world of business and finance.

Table of Contents

ECO-2

BACHELOR'S DEGREE PROGRAMME

Chapter1: Term-End Examination, June, 2013

ELECTIVE COURSE: COMMERCE

ECO-2: ACCOUNTANCY - 1

Time : 2 Hours

Maximum Marks :50

Weightage : 70%

Note: *Attempt* ***any four*** *questions, including question no.* ***1*** *which is compulsory.*

---

1. Answer any two of the following: 7+7

(a) What is consistency concept ? Explain its accounting implications with examples.

(b) Explain the objectives of accounting.

(c) What do you mean by depreciation ? Discuss the factors affecting the amount of depreciation.

(d) Distinguish between provisions and reserves.

2. (a) The Literary Society of Mumbai had received 6+6

Rs. 60,000 in 2010 towards subscription. Further information is :

Subscription for 2009 unpaid on 1.1.2010 were Rs. 4000, Rs. 3800 of which were received in 2010.

Subscription paid in advance on 31.12.2009 were Rs. 1600 and the same on 31.12.2010 were Rs. 2100.

Subscription for 2010 unpaid on 31.12.2010 were Rs. 5,100.

What amount of subscription will be credited to Income and Expenditures account of the year 2010.

(b) What is meant by Receipts and Payments Account ? In what respect does it differ from Income and Expenditure A/C.

3. Raghav Radio & Co., Mumbai sent on consignment to chaddha & Co. Calcutta 100 radiosets, 12

invoiced at Rs. 1,000 each on January 6 2011. Raghav Radio & Co. Paid Rs. 4,000 on the same day for dispatching goods to the consignee. Consignee remitted Rs. 50,000 as an advance by bank draft on 14th January. The consignee is entitled to a commission of 10% on the sale proceeds. On receipts of goods the consignee paid Rs. 2000 for freight and Rs. 4,500 for godown charges. On January 28, Chaddha & Co.. sent an Account sales showing that the radio sets have realized Rs. 1,500/ each. He remits the amount due to Raghav Radio & Co. Pass journal entries in the books of consignor.

4. (a) What is self - Balancing system? State its advantages. 6+6

(b) Discuss the draw backs of single entry system of accounting.

5. Pass journal entries to rectify the following errors. 12

(a) Goods Rs. 4,000 sold on credit to B, no entry was made in books.

(b) No entry was made for purchases returns of Rs. 3,000.

(c) No entry was made for sales returns of Rs. 5,000.

(d) Goods purchased on credit from S Rs. 5,000, was recorded in purchase book as Rs. 500

(e) Sales of Rs. 6,000 to D were recorded as Rs. 600 in sales Book.

(f) Rs. 1,000 Received from Ram has been credited to Shyam's account.

6. Write short notes on any two of the following: 6+6

(a) Provision for doubtful debts

(b) Capital expenditure

(c) Deferred Revenue Expenditure

(d) Cost - concept of Accounting.

ECO-2

BACHELOR'S DEGREE PROGRAMME

Chapter 2: Term-End Examination, December, 2013

ELECIVE COURSE : COMMERCE

ECO-2 : ACCOUNTANCY - 1

Time : 2 Hours

Maximum Marks :50

Weightage : 70%

Note : *Attempt **any four** questions, including question no. **1** which is compulsory.*

---

1. Answer any two of the following: 7+7

(a) What is materiality concept of accounting ? Explain its accounting implications with examples.

(b) Explain the functions of accounting.

(c) State the reasons that lead to disagreement in the balances of Cash Book and Pass Book.

(d) Define Bill of exchange. Prepare an imaginary speciman of a bill of exchange.

2. There was a difference of Rs. 525 in Trial Balance. It was transferred to credit side of suspense Account. Later on, 12

the following errors were discovered. Pass the rectifying journal entries and prepare suspense Account.

(a) An amount of Rs. 375 has been posted on the debit side of commission account instead of Rs. 275.

(b) Goods of Rs. 200 purchased from Ram has been posted to his account as Rs. 250.

(c) Total of Sales Return book was over cast by Rs. 475.

(d) Goods of Rs. 300 were sold to Mahesh, was recorded in purchase book.

3. Distinguish between : 4+4+4

(a) Outstanding expenses and unexpired expenses.

(b) Normal loss and Abnormal loss.

(c) Provision for discount on debtors and provision for discount on creditors.

4. A company had bought machinery for Rs. 1,00,000 including therein a boiler worth Rs. 10,000. 12

Depreciation is provided @ 10% p. a on written down value method. During the 5th year the boiler became useless and the same is sold for Rs. 2,000. Prepare Machine account for 5 years assuming that the Boiler was sold on Is' day of 5th year.

5. (a) Distinguish between consignment and Joint Venture. 6+6

(b) How is valuation of closing stock in consignment accounts done when abnormal and normal losses occur simultaneously ? Explain it with an example.

6. (a) What is a secret reserve ? State the various ways in which it is created.

6+6

(b) Ascertain the cost of goods sold and gross profit from the following figures:

Stock at the beginning

Purchases less Returns

Carriage Inwards

Cartage and Freight

Carriage Outwards

Direct Wages

Sales less Returns

Closing Stock

Rs.

60,000

6,00,000

20,000

10,000

30,000

50,000

12,00,000

40,000

ECO-2

BACHELOR'S DEGREE PROGRAMME

Chapter 3: Term-End Examination, June, 2014

ELECIVE COURSE : COMMERCE

ECO-2 : ACCOUNTANCY - 1

Time : 2 Hours ***Maximum Marks***

:50

Weightage : 70%

Note : *Attempt* ***any four*** *questions, including question no.* ***1*** *which is compulsory.*

---

1. Attempt any two questions from the following :

7+7

(a) What are the advantages of accounting ?

(b) Distinguish between Capital Expenditure and Revenue Expenditure with examples.

(c) Make a clear distinction between 'Sale' and 'Goods Sent on Consignment'.

(d) What is Single Entry System of Book-keeping ? How has Double Entry System removed its limitations ?

2. (a) What are the Rules for recording business transactions in Journal ?

6+6

(b) Pass the Journal Entries for the following :

(i) Credit sales to Sahil, 15,000.

(ii) Cash received from Sahil in full settlement of his account, Rs. 14,750.

(iii) Office rent due 5,000; paid only Rs. 3,000.

(iv) Loss of stock by fire, Rs. 8,500.

3. (a) What are the differences between 'Receipts and Payments Account' and 'Income and Expenditure Account' ? 6+6

(b) Make a distinction between Provisions and Reserves.

4. From the following Ledger balances and adjoining information, you are required to prepare a Trading and Profit

and Loss Account for the year ended on 31st March 2012 and the Balance Sheet as on that date. 12

Particulars	Dr.	Cr.
Opening Stock	40000	-
Purchases	4,10,000	
Sales		4,29,000
Purchases Returns		1,250
Sales Returns	2,500	-
Carriage inward	1,500	-
Carriage Outward	2,500	-
Bank Overdraft	-	21,000
Cash	4,000	
Capital	-	1,27,750
Sundry Creditors	-	37,500
Loans	-	41,375
Investments	10,000	
Accrued incomes	600	
Machinery	47,500	
Drawings	10,000	
Wages	11,000	
Salaries	7,300	
Outstanding Expense		1,000
Prepaid Expenses	750	
Postage	900	
Discount Received		375
Discount Allowed	1,000	
Bad Debts	750	
Debtors	1,00,000	
Interest Paid	3,500	
Interest Received		300
Provision for Bad det		1,750
Furniture and Fixture	7,500	
	6,61,300	**6,61,300**

Other Information :

(a) Unsold Stock 1,10,000

(b) Depreciate Machinery by 10%

(c) Tax Payable 7,500

(d) Accrued Interest on Investment 1,200

4. Pass the necessary Journal entries for the rectification of following accounting errors :
12

(a) Purchase of LCD Projector debited to Purchase Account Rs. 50,000.
(b) Credit Sales of 720 recorded in Sales Journal as Rs. 270.
(c) Credit Sales of 1,500 rupees to Sameer was omitted from being recorded in books.
(d) Sameer had paid Rs. 1,000 but it was credited to Rahim's account.
(e) Discount Allowed column of Cash Book was overcast by Rs. 75.
(f) Sales Book was under cast by Rs. 550.

5. Prepare Machinery Account for the years 2007 to 2011.
12

On 30th June 2007, a business man purchased machinery for Rs. 10,000 and spent on its installation Rs. 1000. It charged depreciation @ 10% annually according to Fixed Instalual method of charging depreciation. On 30-6-2009, he added another machinery costing Rs. 8,000. On 30-6-2011, the machinery purchased on 30-6-2007 was sold for Rs. 5,000.

ECO-2

BACHELOR'S DEGREE PROGRAMME

Chapter 4: Term-End Examination, December, 2014
ELECIVE COURSE : COMMERCE

ECO-2 : ACCOUNTANCY - 1

Time : 2 Hours

Maximum Marks :50

Weightage : 70%

Note : *Attempt* ***any four*** *questions, including question no.* ***1*** *which is compulsory.*

---

1. Attempt any two questions from the following :

7+7

(a) Capital + other liabilities = Total Assets. Explain this Accounting equation with examples.

(b) "Agreement of Trial Balance does not mean that there is no error in account books". Do you agree ? Explain.

(c) Write a clear note on Cash concept Vs Accrual concept of accounting.

(d) Name the parties and their interests in financial statements of a company.

2. Prepare a three column Cash Book from the following transaction :

12

Date	Transaction	Amount
2012		Rs.
Jan. 1	Opening Cash Balance,	5000
	Balance with Bank	30,000
Jan. 2	Borrowing from SBI	50,000
Jan. 5	Cash purchases from Ram	10,000
Jan. 5	Credit purchases	8500
Jan. 10	Cash Sales	12,000
Jan. 15	Deposit in Bank	9000
Jan. 18	Issued cheque to Ram	8000
Jan. 20	Bad debt recovered	5000
Jan. 22	Received cash from A	750
Jan. 25	Withdrawal from Bank for business pur	4500
Jan. 26	Withdrew cash for personal use	2000
Jan. 27	Received cheque from Sham and deposi bank	5000
Jan. 28	Paid monthly Rent by cheque	3000
Jan. 29	Received cash from Soni, 2910 in full s of	3000
Jan. 30	Paid to Ram Rs. 1950 in full settlement account of	2000
Jan. 30	Issue salary cheque	4500
Jan. 30	Paid Installment of loan by cheque	5500

3. (a) State the entries that are usually passed for recording transactions in consignor's and consignee's books. 6+6

(b) What steps are required to be taken to convert single entry into double entry system of book keeping ? Explain.

4. What is an Accommodation Bill of Exchange ? Explain with an example. 4+8

On 1st Jan. 2012, X draws a bill amounting to Rs. 12000 for 3 months, on Y for mutual benefit. Y accepts the bill and return to X who discounted the same with his banker @ 12% per annum and remitted half of the proceeds to Y. On due date X sends the requisite amount to Y who met the bill on maturity. Pass the necessary entries in the books of X and Y.

1. (a) Where will you show the following items in the Final Accounts of a sole proprietor. 8+4

(i) Loss by fire

(ii) Transfer of some profit to General Reserve

(iii) Commission paid to agents

(iv) Drawings by the proprietor

(v) Outstanding Rent

(vi) Sales returns

(vii) Manufacturing expenses

(viii) Samples distributed

(b) List the errors which do not effect the agreement of Trial Balance.

2. (a) From the following Receipts and Payments Account of a club, prepare Income and Expenditure Account 8+4

for the year ended as on Dec. 31, 2011. Receipt and Payment Account for the year ending Dec. 31, 2011

Receipts	Rs.	Payments	Rs.
Balance b/d	3,500	General expenses	900
Subscription :		Salary	16,000
2010	1,800	Postage	1,300
2011	70,000	Electricity bill	7,800
2012	3,200	Furniture	26,500
Sale of old books (cost Rs. 3,200)	2,000	Books	13,000
Rent from use of Hall	17,000	Newspapers	600
Sale of old News papers	400	Meeting expenses	7,200
Profit from entertainment programme	7,300	TV set	16,000
		Balance c/d	15,900
	1,05,200		1,05,200

Additional Information :

(i) The club has 100 members each paying an annual subscription of Rs. 900. Subscription outstanding on Dec 31, 2010, were Rs. 3600.

(ii) On Dec. 31, 2011, salary outstanding accounted to Rs. 1000, salary paid included Rs. 1000 for the year 2010.

(b) How do professionals account for their outstanding professional fees ?

ECO-2

BACHELOR'S DEGREE PROGRAMME

Chapter 5: Term-End Examination, June , 2015
ELECIVE COURSE : COMMERCE

ECO-2 : ACCOUNTANCY - 1

Time : 2 Hours ***Maximum Marks***

:50

Weightage : 70%

Note : *Attempt* ***any four*** *questions, including question no.* ***1*** *which is* ***compulsory.***

---

1. Answer any two of the following :

7+7

(a) Name the parties interested in Accounting information and state their basic interests there in.

(b) Explain with example the 'Cost Concept' and 'Dual Aspect Concept'.

(c) "Single entry book-keeping is an incomplete system". Do you agree ? Explain.

(d) Explain the method of valuation of unsold stock for calculating fair profit on consignment.

2. (a) What is Bank Reconciliation Statement ? What are its advantages ?

6+6

(b) On 31St Dec. 2012, the Cash Book of Mr. Karamat Ali showed a debit balance of 5,850. Prepare the Bank Reconciliation statement to work out the passbook balance from the following information :

(i) Cheques amounting to 1,350 issued in mid December have not been presented for payment till 31-12-12.

(ii) A cheque of 900 was deposited but it was collected in the first week of January.

(iii) Dividend collected by bank, 390 has not been shown in Cash book.

(iv) 225 deposited by a customer direct in the bank account of the account holder.

(v) Bank charges, 45 appeared only in the pass book.

(vi) A cheque of 120 entered in Cash Book but it was not sent to bank for collection.

Salaries	36,000	
Rent	26,250	
Interest paid on bank loan	11,250	
Discount	3,750	
Bad debt	3,750	
Interest received		7,125
Cash in hand	16,125	
Cash at Bank	41,250	
Investments	56,250	
Debtors	1,14,000	
Goodwill	37,500	
Creditors		1,50,000
B/R and B/P	15,000	11,250
Bank Loan		1,87,500
	20,97,375	**20,97,375**

3. Prepare Final Accounts from the following Trial Balance which belong to financial year ending on 31st December 2012 12

Other Information :

(a) Stock as on 31-12-2012, 13,500

(b) Make a provision for doubtful debts @ 5%

(c) Accrued interest on investment, 1,200

(d) Depreciate Machinery by 10% and Furniture by 10%

4. Ram and Raheem entered into a contract to construct a building for 10,00,000. Ram was entrusted to maintain 12

joint venture accounts and also to look after the joint venture business. He was entitled to a commission of 5% on contract price, in addition to a profit in a ratio of 4 : 3. Raheem paid his share of contribution of 4,00,000. Ram purchased construction material for 7,25,000 and paid other expenses, 25,000. Ram also contributed material from his own stock worth 40,000. Stock remaining unconsumed was taken over by Raheem for 50,000. Record the above transactions in the Journal of Ram and show the Joint Venture Account and Raheem's personal account as the working notes.

5. Comment on any two of the following statements :

6+6

(a) Income and Expenditure Account is different from Profit and Loss Account.

(b) Trial Balance is not the conclusive proof a accuracy of books.

(c) Accounting equation is based on Dual concept of Book-keeping.

6. (a) From the following particulars taken from the Cash Book of a club prepare a Receipts

6+6

and Payments Account for the year ending 31-3-2013.

ECO-2

Chapter 6: Term-End Examination, December, 2015
ELECIVE COURSE : COMMERCE
ECO-2 : ACCOUNTANCY - 1

Time : 2 Hours

Maximum Marks :50

Weightage : 70%

Note : *Attempt* ***any four*** *questions, including question no.* ***1*** *which is* ***compulsory.***

---

1. Answer any two of the following : 7+7

(a) Distinguish between Single Entry System and Double Entry System of Accounting.

(b) What is the difference between Receipts and Payment Account and Income and Expenditure Account ? Explain.

(c) Explain the concepts of 'Conservatism and 'Consistency' with examples.

(d) State the difference between Capital Expenditure and Revenue Expenditure.

2. (a) What is 'Net Worth' ? How is it computed ? Explain with an example.
6+6

(b) What do you understand by Self-Balancing System ? State its advantages.

2. On 1st April, 2013 a firm of Sportswear, Delhi sent a consignment of 500 swimming suits to M/s Ram Niwas 12
and Sons of Kanpur (consignee) valuing Z 1,25,000. The consignor incurred anamount of Z 1500 in sending the goods to the consignee. At the end of the month, the consignee sent a statement of sales showing that 400 suits were sold @ Z 350 per suit and his selling expenses amounted to Z 8000. The consignee is entitled for a commission of Z 25 per suit sold. The unsold stock is to be valued at cost plus proportionate expenses. The consignee had also spent

Z 500 on consignment received. You are required to show necessary ledger accounts in the books of the consignor.

3. From the following Ledger Balances extracted from the books of a proprietor as on 31st March, 2013 prepare the 12

Trading and Profit and Loss Account for the year ending on 31-03-2013 and also the Balance Sheet after taking into account the following additional information :

Name of Ledger Account	Debit (Rs)	Credit (Rs)
Capital		8,00,000
Sales		15,00,000
Return Inward	35,000	
Purchases	7,65,000	
Return Outward		22,000
Stock (1-4-2012)	80,000	
Land and Building	8,00,000	
Plant and Machinery	4,00,000	
Furniture and Fixtures	1,50,000	
Wages	70,000	
Carriage Inward	15,000	
Salaries	48,000	
Rent	35,000	
Interest on Loan	15,000	
Discount	5,000	
Bad Debts	5,000	
Interest on Investment		9,500
Cash in Hand	21,500	
Cash at Bank	55,000	
Investments	75,000	
Debtors	1,52,000	
Creditors		2,00,000
Bills Receivable and Payable	20,000	15,000
Loan		2,50,000
Total	27,96,500	27,96,500

Additional Information :

(a) Unsold stock on 31-3-2013, Z 1,75,000.

(b) Depreciate : Plant and Machinery @ 15%

Furniture and Fixtures @ 15%.

(c) Provide Bad debt Reserve @ 5%.

(d) Outstanding Rent, 13,000.

4.On January 1, 2010, a firm purchased a Machine for Z 75,000 and spent Z 5,000 on its erection. On1st July, the 12

same year, a second machine was purchased for Z 40,000. On 1st July 2011, the firm sold the machine which had been purchased on 1-1-2010, for Z 55,000. On July 1, 2012, a new plant costing Rs. 60,000 was added and the machinery purchased on 1st July 2010 was disposed off for Rs 30,000. Firm charges depreciation annually @ 10% on fixed instalment basis. Prepare Machinery Account for 3-years showing balance as it would appear on 1-1-2013.

5. Write short notes on any two of the following : 6+6

(a) Joint Venture as a temporary partnership.

(b) Secret reserves.

(c) Selection of a method of charging depreciation.

(d) Types of Assets.

ECO-2

BACHELOR'S DEGREE PROGRAMME

Chapter 7: Term-End Examination, June, 2016
ELECIVE COURSE : COMMERCE

ECO-2 : ACCOUNTANCY - 1

Time : 2 Hours

Maximum Marks :50

Weightage : 70%

Note : *Attempt **any four** questions, including question no. **1** which is **compulsory.***

---

1. Attempt any two questions from the following :
7+7

(a) State the essential features of Receipts and Payments Account.

(b) Discuss the drawbacks of Single Entry System of accounting.

(c) Distinguish between 'consignment' and 'Joint Venture'.

(d) Describe briefly the procedure for locating errors.

2. On 1st April, 2010, Gama Ltd. purchased a machine for 3,90,000 and spent Z 10,000 for its installation. 12
On 1st November, 2011, company purchased another machine for 1,00,000 and spent 20,000 on its overhauling. On 30th September, 2012, the machine purchased in 2010 was sold at a loss of Z 1,27,800. The company charges depreciation @ 10% p.a. on written down value basis. Accounts are closed on 31st March every year. Prepare machine account up to 31st March 2013.

3. (a) Why is provision for doubtful debts created ? How is it shown in the Balance Sheet if it is given in 6+6

(i) Adjustments and

(ii) in trial balance ?

(b) Explain the role of Suspense Account in rectifying one sided errors with suitable examples.

4. On 1st September, 2013 Shri Gupta of Delhi sent 500 cases of goods @ 150 each to Shri Jha of Ranchi to be sold 8+4

on his account at his risk for 7.5% commission and 2.5% del-credere commission and incurred 5,500 as expenses. 20,000 advance has been received on 31st December, 2013. Shri Jha sent an account sales disclosing that 300 cases have been sold for 230 each for cash and another 100 cases at 220 each on credit. He incurred 1,750 as selling expenses. He sends a bank draft for the net amount due. Prepare Consignment Account and Consignee Account in the books of Shri Gupta.

5. Siyaram keeps incomplete records from the following, calculate total sales made during the period from 1st January, 2013 to 31st December 2013 : 12

Description	Amount (Rs.)
Bills Receivables in the beginning	7,800
Bills Receivables encashed during the year	20,900
Debtors (1.1.2013)	30,800
Cash received from debtors	70,000
Bad-debts written off	2,800
Return inwards	8,700
Bills Receivables dishonoured	1,800
Bills Receivables at the end	25,500
Cash sales	40,900
Closing balance of Debtors	6,100

(a) What is Trial Balance ? Explain how is it prepared. 6+6

(b) State any six reasons of disagreement between the balances shown by Cash Book and Pass Book.

ECO-2

BACHELOR'S DEGREE PROGRAMME

Chapter 8: Term-End Examination, December, 2016
ELECIVE COURSE : COMMERCE

ECO-2 : ACCOUNTANCY - 1

Time : 2 Hours

Maximum Marks :50

Weightage : 70%

Note : *Attempt* ***any four*** *questions, including question no.* ***1*** *which is* ***compulsory.***

---

1. Attempt any two questions from the following :

7+7

(a) Define accounting and explain its objectives.

(b) What are the advantages of Maintaining Petty Cash Book ? Explain the imprest system of Maintaining Petty Cash.

(c) Distinguish between Sectional Balancing and Self-balancing.

(d) Explain deferred revenue expenditure with examples.

2. Rectify the following errors by making a Journal entry :

12

i. Machine purchased for Rs 5,000 has been debited to purchase A/c.

ii. 3,000 being the sale proceeds of an old furniture has been credited to sales A/c.

iii. Goods purchased from Sanjay for 2,000 was recorded as Rs 200 only.

iv. Goods sold to Mohan for 380 on credit was recorded as Rs 830.

v. 800 paid for rent wrongly debited to landlord's A/c.

vi. No entry has been made for sales return of Rs 450.

3. Ajay and Vijay were partners in a joint venture, sharing profit and losses equally. Ajay supplied goods to the value of Rs 2,500 and incurred expenses amounting to Rs 250. Vijay supplied goods to the value of Rs 2,000 and incurred expenses amounting to Rs 200. Vijay sold the entire goods on the behalf of the joint venture and realized Rs 6,000. Vijay was entitled to commission of 5% on sales. Vijay settled his account by bank draft. Show Joint venture account and Ajay's Account in the books of Vijay.

12

4. Surya Ltd. purchased a machine for Rs 40,000 on its July 2010. Depreciation is provided @ 10% on the diminishing balance method. On Its October 2012, a part of the machine costing Rs 10,000 was found damaged and disposed off for ! 6,000. On the same date a new machine at a cost of Rs 15,000 was purchased. Prepare machine A/c from 2010 to 2013. The accounts are closed on 31st December each year. 12

5.Write short notes on any two of the following :

6+6

(a) Accrued Income

(b) Capital Expenditure

(c) Bank Reconciliation Statement

(d) Contingent Liabilities

6. (a) State the features of Income and Expenditure account.

6+6

(b) What is meant by Incomplete Records ? What are their limitations ?

ECO-2

BACHELOR'S DEGREE PROGRAMME

Chapter 9: Term-End Examination, June, 2017
ELECIVE COURSE : COMMERCE

ECO-2 : ACCOUNTANCY - 1

Time : 2 Hours *Maximum Marks*

:50

Weightage : 70%

Note : *Attempt* ***any four*** *questions, including question no.* ***1*** *which is* ***compulsory.***

---

1. Attempt any two questions from the following : 7+7

   (a) Explain briefly the 'conservatism concept' of accounting with examples.

   (b) State the advantages of maintaining a Petty Cash Book.

   (c) Describe the utility of debit note and credit note.

   (d) State the transactions recorded in Bills Receivable and Bills Payable Journals.

2. (a) What do you understand by self-balancing system ? State its advantages.
6+6

   (b) Explain the drawbacks of Single Entry System of accounting.

3. (a) The balance of Machine Account on January 1, 2013 was Z 10,00,000. New machines were purchased, 8+4
one on 1-10-2013 for Rs 50,000 and the other on 1-7-2014 for Rs 1,00,000. On 1-4-2015, a machine whose book value had been Rs 1,50,000 on 1-1-2013 was sold for Rs 80,000 and the entire amount was credited to Machine Account. Depreciation had been charged at 10% p.a. on straight line method. Show Machine Account from 1.1.2013 to 31-12-2015.

(a) Distinguish between Provisions and Reserves.

4.There was a difference of Rs 5,250 in a Trial Balance. It had been transferred to the credit side of Suspense Account. Later on, the following errors were discovered.

12

(a) An amount of Rs 3,750 had been posted on the debit side of Commission Account instead of Rs 2,750.

(b) Goods worth Rs 2,000 purchased from if had been posted to his account as Rs 2,500.

(c) Total of Sales Returns Book was overcast by Rs 4,750.

(d) Goods worth Rs 3,000 sold to Mahesh was recorded in Purchases Book. Pass the necessary rectifying journal entries and prepare the Suspense Account.

5. (a) Distinguish between Joint Venture and Partnership.

4+8

(b) Philips Radio Company, Mumbai consigned 100 transistors to their agents Paul Radios, Delhi. The cost price of each transistor was 750. The consignors paid 2,000 for freight, 500 for cartage and 4,000 for insurance. Five transistors were totally destroyed in transit. The insurance claim of 3,000 was admitted by the insurance company. The consignee took the delivery of 95 transistors and spent 6,850 on cartage and godown rent. They sold all the transistors at 1,000 each. Paul Radios are entitled to a commission of 5% on sales. Prepare consignment A/c and AbnormalLoss A/c in the books of the consignors.

6. (a) Why is an Income and Expenditure Account termed as Receipt and Expenditure Account in case of 6+6

professiorials? How do theyaccount for the outstanding fees ?

(b)From the following information prepare the General Ledger Adjustment Account in Creditors' Ledger :

Description	Amount (Rs.)
Opening Balance of Sundry Creditors	2,80,100
Credit Purchases	2,76,000
Payment to Creditors	2,65,000
Discount Allowed by Creditors	18,500
Returns Outwards	22,400
Bills Payable Accepted	53,000
Bills Payable Dishonoured	5,000

ECO-2

BACHELOR'S DEGREE PROGRAMME

Chapter 10: Term-End Examination, December, 2017

ELECIVE COURSE : COMMERCE

ECO-2 : ACCOUNTANCY - 1

Time : 2 Hours

Maximum Marks :50

Weightage : 70%

Note : *Attempt* ***any four*** *questions, including question no.* ***1*** *which is* ***compulsory.***

---

1. Attempt any two questions from the following :

   7+7

(a) What do you understand by Dual Aspect Concept. Explain its accounting implications.

(b) What do you mean by Trial Balance ? State the errors which are not disclosed by the trial balance.

(c) What is Bank Reconciliation Statement ? State its advantages.

(d) Prepare an imaginary specimen of a bill of exchange, and state the purpose of noting thereon.

2. (a) State the procedure to be followed for preparing Receipts and Payments Account from the Income and Expenditure Account.

   6+6

(b) The following items relate to a sports club. Show how subscriptions will appear in the Income and Expenditure Account of the club for the year 2014-15 and its Balance Sheet as on 31-3-2015.

	Amount (Rs.)
Subscriptions received during the year 2014-15	1,84,000
Subscriptions outstanding as on 31-03-2014	18,000
Subscriptions received in advance as on 31-03-2014	11,600
Subscriptions outstanding as on 31-03-2015	13,600
Subscriptions received in advance as on 31-03-2015	6,000

3. Mr. Ahuja did not keep proper books of accounts. However, the following information is available from his records, for the year ending March 31st, 2015 : 12

	As on 31-03-2014 (Rs.)	As on 31-03-2015 (Rs.)
Cash in hand and at bank	20,000	36,000
Stock on hand	3,00,000	2,60,000
Sundry Debtors	2,50,000	2,90,000
Machinery	4,00,000	4,00,000
Sundry Creditors	2,00,000	1,85,000

Cash Received	Amount (Rs.)	Cash Paid	Amount (Rs.)
Balance b/d	20,000	Cash paid to Creditors	5,50,000
Cash received from Debtors	8,65,000	Wages	1,01,000
Cash Sales	42,000	Sundry Expenses	66,000
Sale of Old Newspaper	2,000	Buildings Purchased	1,50,000
Loan from Mrs. Ahuja (@ 6% p.a. on 1-10-14)	20,000	Drawings	46,000
		Balance c/d	36,000
	9,49,000	Total Cash Paid	9,49,000

Additional Information :

(a) During the year Z 5,000 had to be written off as bad.

(b) Provide Depreciation @ 15% on machinery.

(c) Outstanding expenses were 8,000.

Prepare Ahuja's Trading and Profit & Loss Account for the year ending March 31st, 2015 and the Balance sheet as on that date.

4 Write short notes on the following :

4+4+4

(a) Depletion Method of Providing Depreciation.

(b) Imprest system of cash.

(c) Sinking Fund to Repay a Liability.

5. (a) Explain different types of errors with suitable examples. Prepare Manufacturing Account from the following data relating to the year ended on 31st December, 2014.

6+6

	Amount (Rs.)
Raw materials purchased	4,00,000
Stock of raw materials on 1.1.2014	40,000
Work-in-Progress on 1.1.2014	20,000
Factory Wages	60,000
Factory Rent	20,000
Fuel & Power	8,000
Carriage Inwards	4,000
Repairs of Plant	8,000
Depreciation of plant	20,000
Sale of Scrap	-2,000
Stock of raw materials on 31-12-2014	-80,000
Stock of Work-in-Progress on 31-12-2014	30,000

6. (a) A and B entered into a joint venture agreeing to share profits and losses equally. The following transactions took place during the course of the venture.

8+4

A Bought goods for cash	2,50,000
B Bought goods for cash	7,00,000
A Paid storage charges	50,000
B Paid freight & insurance	80,000
B Sold goods for cash	7,00,000
B Received 3% commission on sales made by him	(Amount not provided)
Sales made by A	5,00,000
Commission payable to A	15,000
B Took over the unsold stock	56,000

Prepare the necessary ledger accounts in the books of A, assuming that the accounts have been finally settled between them.

(b) Distinguish between normal and abnormal loss with an example.

ECO-2

BACHELOR'S DEGREE PROGRAMME

Chapter 11: Term-End Examination, June, 2018
ELECIVE COURSE : COMMERCE

ECO-2 : ACCOUNTANCY - 1

Time : 2 Hours

Maximum Marks :50

Weightage : 70%

Note : *Attempt* ***any four*** *questions, including question no.* ***1*** *which is* ***compulsory.***

---

1. Attempt any two questions from the following :

7+7

(a) What is Accounting ? Explain its main objectives.

(b) Enumerate the accounting concepts which relate to final accounts, and explain any one of these with its accounting implications.

(c) How do professionals account for outstanding fees ?

(d) How does debit note differ from credit note ? State the utility of these notes.

2. Rectify the following errors by journal entries assuming that a suspense account had been opened : 12

(a) 5,400 received from M. Mehta were posted to the debit side of his account.

(b) 1,000 being purchase returns were posted to the debit of Purchases Account.

(c) 5,740 paid for repairs of a motor car were debited to the Motor Car Account as 1,740.

(d) Purchase of a machine for 60,000 was recorded in the Purchases Book.

(e) A sale of goods for 3,500 to Sethi was entered in the Sales Book at 5,300.

(f) 5,000 paid towards wages for installing a machine was debited to Wages Account.

3. (a) What is Single Entry System ? State its salient features.

6+6

(b) From the following particulars relating to Bhasin Brothers for the year 2015-16 ascertain their credit sales for the year :

	Amount (Rs.)
Debtors as on 1-4-2015	1,20,000
Returns Inwards	50,000
Cash received from debtors	4,50,000
Discount allowed to debtors	30,000
Bills Receivable accepted by debtors	1,70,000
Bad Debts	15,000
Debtors as on 31-3-2016	1,00,000
Bills Receivable dishonoured	35,000

4. (a) What do you mean by Sectional Balancing ? How does it differ from self-balancing ?

6+6

(b) Differentiate between provisions and reserves.

5. From the following Receipts and Payments Account and Balance Sheet of a Club prepare the Income and Expenditure Account for the year ending 31 December, 2015 and the Balance Sheet as on that date. 12

Receipts and Payments A/c

For the Year Ending Dec. 31, 2015

	Amount (Rs.)		Amount (Rs.)
Balance b/d	10,00,000	Expenses	
Subscriptions		2014	1,40,000
2014	38,000	2015	2,00,000
2015	2,10,000	Total Expenses	3,40,000
2016	15,000	Leasehold Land	4,00,000
Total Subscriptions	2,63,000	Interest Paid	40,000
Entrance Fees	80,000	Refreshment Exp.	2,00,000
Locker Rent	70,000	Balance c/d	8,33,000
Income From Refreshments	4,00,000		
Total Receipts	18,13,000	Total Payments	18,13,000

Balance Sheet as on Dec. 31, 2014
(Opening for 2015)

Liabilities	Rs	Assets	Rs
Capital Fund	33,62,000	Bldgs.	30,00,000
Subs. recd. in advance	60,000	Cash in hand	10,00,000
Subs. Outstanding	1,40,000	Locker Rent	24,000
Outstanding Expenses	38,000	Loan	5,00,000
Loan	5,00,000		
Total Liabilities	40,62,000	Total Assets	40,62,000

Adjustments :

(a) Exp. Outstanding 31-12-2015 50,000

(b) Subs. Outstanding 31-12-2015 80,000

(c) Salary due but not paid upto 31-12-2015 20,000

(d) Depreciation of 2,00,000 to be charged on buildings.

(e) Entrance fees are to be capitalised.

6. (a) R and S entered into a contract for constructing a building for 4,00,000. R and S contributed 2,00,000 and 1,50,000 respectively. They agreed to share profits and losses in the ratio of 4 : 3. It was decided that the work will be looked after by R who will be paid 5% commission on contract price in addition to his share of profits. R purchased the necessary materials for 3,20,000 and paid 9,000 for expenses. R also contributed building materials from his own stock worth 20,000. 5,000 remained to be paid for wages. S took over the stock of materials for an agreed value of 16,000. The building was completed and the contract money was duly received. Prepare Joint Venture A/c in the books of R. 8+4

(b) Distinguish between Account Sales and Invoice.

ECO-2

BACHELOR'S DEGREE PROGRAMME

Chapter 12: Term-End Examination, December, 2018
ELECIVE COURSE : COMMERCE

ECO-2 : ACCOUNTANCY - 1

Time : 2 Hours

Maximum Marks :50

Weightage : 70%

Note : *Attempt* ***any four*** *questions, including question no.* ***1*** *which is* ***compulsory.***

---

1. Attempt any two questions from the following :

7+7

(a) Enumerate the accounting concepts which guide the accountant at recording stage, and czr (Y) explain any one of these with its accounting implications.

(b) Distinguish between capital reserves and revenue reserves.

(c) State the expenses that are not considered while valuing unsold stock lying with the consignee. .

(d) What is self-balancing system ? State its advantages

2. On 30th April, 2016 the Cash Book of Srikanth showed an overdraft of 37,200. Prepare a Bank Reconciliation Statement using the following information :

12

(a) Out of two cheques issued to Kumar on April 25, 2016 (One for 1,500 and another for 3,750) the cheque for 3,750 was cashed on May 5, 2016.

(b) A wrong credit for 375 relating to some other account was found in the Pass-Book.

(c) Three cheques for 4,500, 6,000 and 7,500 were deposited in the bank on April 22, 2016. Only the cheque for 6,000 was collected by Bank upto April 30, 2016.

(d) There was a debit of 1,200 for interest and 225 for bank charges in the Pass-Book only.

(e) The Pass-Book showed that the bank had collected 9,000 as interest on securities. But there was no entry found in the Cash Book for the same.

(f) A bill receivable for 7,500 which had been discounted with the bank in March, 2016 was dishonoured on April 28, 2016. But it was debited in the Pass-Book only.

3. The Trial Balance of firm showed the following balances as on December 31, 2015 :

6+6

Description	Amount (Rs.)
Salaries	10,000
Wages (Indirect)	20,000
Rent Received	6,600
Commission Received	2,000
Interest on Investments	6,000

Additional Information :

(a) Salaries amounting to 2,000 were outstanding.

(b) Wages include 1,500 paid in advance.

(c) Interest on investments include 1,200 for the month of January, 2016.

(d) Rent 600 for the month of December, 2015 has not yet been received.

Gross Profit for the year amounted to 40,000 and other expenses 10,000. Pass journal entries for the adjustments and prepare Profit and Loss A/c for the year ending December 31, 2015.

4. Distinguish between :

4+4+4

(a) Outstanding expenses and Unexpired expenses.

(b) Bill of Exchange and Promissory Note.

(c) Provision for Discount on Debtors and Provision for Discount on Creditors.

5. Vanaspati Ltd. consigned 500 kg of vanaspati ghee to Ashoka Brothers, Chandigarh. Each kg of ghee cost 80. Vanaspati Ltd. paid 50 for carriage, i 250 for packing and 200 for insurance in transit. After three months from the date of consignment of goods, Ashoka Brothers reported that

350 kg of ghee had been sold @ 95 per kg and expenses incurred were 500 on godown rent and 750 on salesman's salary. Ashoka Brothers are entitled to a commission of 5% on sales. 50 kg of ghee was accidentally destroyed in the godown. Insurance claim of 3,500 was admitted. Prepare the necessary accounts in the books of Vanaspati Ltd.

12

6.Write short notes on the following : 4+4+4

(a) Diminishing Balance Method of providing Depreciation.

(b) Sinking Fund to Repay a Liability. (c) Memorandum Trading Account.

ECO-2

BACHELOR'S DEGREE PROGRAMME

Chapter 13: Term-End Examination, June, 2019
ELECIVE COURSE : COMMERCE

ECO-2 : ACCOUNTANCY - 1

Time : 2 Hours

Maximum Marks :50

Weightage : 70%

Note : *Attempt **any four** questions, including question no. **1** which is **compulsory.***

---

1. Attempt any two questions from the following

7+7=14

(a) Define Accounting and state its limitations.

(b) Who are interested in accounting information ? What are their needs ?

(c) State the most commonly used instruments of credit. Which are the various parties to a Bill of Exchange ?

(d) What are the different types of cash books used in business ? Explain the use of any one of these.

2. (a) Identify the types of errors which are usually committed in the process of accounting.

[4]

(a) Rectify the following errors assuming that a Suspense Account had been opened :

(i) A purchase of Rs. 8,000 from 'B' on credit was debited to him.

(ii) An amount of Rs. 300 received from Mr. C was debited to his account.

(iii) A credit sale of Rs. 500 to Ramesh was credited to his account.

(iv) A sale of Rs. 3,000 to Goel was debited to his account as Rs. 8,000. Pass necessary rectifying journal entries. [8]

3. Rohan and Sohan entered into a contract to construct a building for Rs. 40,00,000. Rohan and Sohan contributed Rs. 20,00,000 and Rs. 15,00,000 respectively. They agreed to share profits and losses in the ratio of 4 : 3. It was decided that the work will be looked after by Rohan who will be paid 5 per cent commission on contract price in addition to his share of profits. Rohan purchased the necessary materials for Rs. 32,00,000 and paid Rs. 90,000 for expenses. Rohan also contributed building materials from his own stock worth Rs. 2,00,000. Rs. 50,000 remained to be paid for wages. Sohan took over the stock of materials for an agreed valuation of Rs. 1,60,000. The building was completed and the contract money was duly received. Show the Joint Venture Account and Sohan's Account in the books of Rohan assuming that the outstanding wages were paid by Rohan.

[12]

4. (a) Explain briefly the Self-Balancing System of Accounting. Also state its advantages.

[6]

(b) What is Single Entry System ? Distinguish it from Double Entry System.

[6]

5. (a) Distinguish between Capital Reserve and Revenue Reserve.

[4]

(b) Mohan and Sons purchased a machine for Rs. 50,00,000 on April 1, 2013. The machinery was depreciated at 10 per cent under the straight line method. On April 1, 2016, they changed the method of depreciation from straight line method to written down value method without changing the rate and effective from the beginning. Show the Machinery Account from April 1, 2013 to March 31, 2017. [8]

6.(a) Show how will you deal with the following items while preparing the final accounts of a non-trading concern : [4]

Donation when purpose is not mentioned.

Receipts for Tournament Fund.

(b) From the following particulars, draw up a General Ledger Adjustment Account in the Debtors Ledger : [8]

	Amount (Rs.)
Opening Balance	12,200
Credit Sales	37,200
Cash Received from Debtors	20,050
Sales Returns	3,170
Discount Allowed	1,300
Bad Debts Written-off	3,710
Allowances	420
Bills Receivable Received	1,300
Bills Receivable Dishonored	500

ECO-2

BACHELOR'S DEGREE PROGRAMME

Chapter 14: Term-End Examination, December, 2020

ELECIVE COURSE : COMMERCE

ECO-2 : ACCOUNTANCY - 1

Time : 2 Hours

Maximum Marks :50

Weightage : 70%

Note : *Attempt any* ***four*** *questions. Questions no. 1 is compulsory.*

---

1. Attempt any two from the following :

7 + 7

(a) State the advantages of Self-balancing system.

(b) Write a note on 'cost concept' of Accounting.

(c) Explain the features of consignment.

(d) Distinguish between 'Provision' and 'Reserve'.

2. What are the essential features of Receipts and Payments Account ? How does it differ from Cash Book ? Explain.

6 + 6

3. What are various types of errors which are usually committed in the process of accounting ? Explain with examples.

6 + 6

3. Give journal entries for the following adjustments :

2+2+3+2+3

(a) Interest received in advance Rs. 600

(b) Interest on drawing Rs. 1,200

(c) Provision for discount on creditors Rs. 200

(d) Loss of goods by theft Rs. 8,500

(e) Drawing of goods by proprietor Rs. 750

4. Differentiate between :

6 + 6

(i) 'Joint venture' and 'Consignment'

(ii) 'Joint venture' and 'Partnership'

5. How would you deal with the following items while preparing the final accounts of a nontrading concern ? 2 × 6

(a) Legacy

(b) Donation when purpose is not mentioned

(c) Life membership fees

(d) Receipts for Tournament Fund

(e) Sales of used sports material

(f) Entrance fees

ECO-2

BACHELOR'S DEGREE PROGRAMME

Chapter 15: Term-End Examination, June, 2021

ELECIVE COURSE : COMMERCE

ECO-2 : ACCOUNTANCY - 1

Time : 2 Hours

Maximum Marks :50

Weightage : 70%

Note : *Attempt any four questions including Question No. 1 which is compulsory*

---

1. Attempt any two of the following questions : 2x7=14

(a) What are the objectives of Accounting ? Name the different parties interested in accounting information.

(b) What do you understand by an Opening Entry ? How is an opening entry posted into the ledger ?

(c) State the various causes of disagreement between the balances shown by Cash Book and Pass Book.

(d) Differentiate between a Bill of Exchange and a Promissory Note. State their importance for modern business.

2.(a) Is Trial Balance a conclusive proof of the accuracy of the books of accounts ? If not, discuss the errors which are not disclosed by the Trial Balance.

6

(b) An extract from a trader's Trial Balance on March 31, 2017 is given below:

Name of the Account	Dr.	Cr.
Sundry Debtors	12,80,000	
Bad Debts	80,000	
Provision for Bad Debts		1,40,000

Adjustments : Write off further bad debts < 40,000 and create a provision for doubtful debts at 5 per cent on debtors. Pass the necessary Journal entries and show Bad Debts and Provision for Bad Debts Accounts. 6

3. Philips Radio & Company, Delhi sent one consignment to Chander & Company, Mumbai containing 100 radio sets, invoiced at < 100 each on January 6, 2017. Phillips Radio & Company paid < 1,000 on the same day for dispatching goods to the consignee. The consignee remitted < 5,000 as an advance by bank draft on January 14. The consignee is entitled to a commission of 10% on the sale proceeds. On receipt of the goods, the consignee paid < 1,000 for freight and < 500 for godown charges. On January 28, Chander & Company sold the goods at < 200 per radio set and remitted the amount due to Phillips Radio & Company. Pass Journal entries and prepare necessary ledger accounts in the books of the consignor.
12

4. Mahesh keeps his books on single entry system. His position on March 31, 2016 was as follows :

Description	Amount (Rs.)
Cash in hand	2,400
Cash at bank	25,500
Debtors	18,400
Stock	28,600
Furniture	5,000
Creditors	18,700
Expenses Outstanding	2,000

On October 1, 2016 Mahesh introduced < 10,000 as additional capital in the business out of which a machine costing < 5,000 was purchased for the business. His drawings during the year totalled < 2,000.

On March 31, 2017 his position was as follows :

Description	Amount (Rs.)
Cash in hand	2,600
Cash at bank	27,500
Debtors	24,200
Stock	31,500
Furniture	4,500
Creditors	20,200
Prepaid Insurance	200

Prepare the necessary Statements of Affairs and Statement of Profit for the year ending March 31, 2017 and ascertain the profit or loss.

12

5. (a) Explain the meaning and accounting treatment of the terms 'Subscriptions' and 'Legacy' while preparing the final accounts of a non-trading concern.

4

(b) Mohan and Sons purchased machinery for < 25,00,000 on April 1, 2013. The machinery was depreciated at 10 per cent per year under the straight line method. On April 1, 2016, they changed the method of depreciation from straight line method to written down value method of depreciation without changing the rate. Show the Machinery Account from April 1, 2013 to March 31, 2017. 8

6. Write short notes on any three of the following :

3x4=12

(a) Difference between Joint Venture and Partnership

(b) Going Concern Concept

(c) Self-Balancing System

(d) Capital Reserve and Revenue Reserve

(e) Straight Line Method of Depreciation

ECO-2

BACHELOR'S DEGREE PROGRAMME

Chapter 16: Term-End Examination, June, 2021
ELECIVE COURSE : COMMERCE

ECO-2 : ACCOUNTANCY - 1

Time : 2 Hours

Maximum Marks :50

Weightage : 70%

Note : *Attempt any four questions including Question No. 1 which is compulsory*

---

1. Attempt any two of the following questions :

7×2=14

(a) Define accounting and explain its scope.

(b) What is Journal Proper ? What entries are usually recorded in the Journal Proper ?

(c) What is Bank Reconciliation Statement ? How is it prepared ?

(d) What is the purpose of noting on the bill ? Is it necessary in case of a Promissory Note ?

2. (a) Distinguish between cash basis and accrual basis of accounting. Why do you consider accrual basis more

rational ? Discuss.

6

(b) The following were the balances of assets as on January 1, 2017 :

Plant and Machinery ` 12,00,000

Furniture ` 1,80,000

A new machinery costing ` 3,00,000 was acquired on July 1, 2017. Depreciation is to be provided on plant and machinery at 10% and on furniture at 5% p. a. Show how depreciation will be shown in the final accounts. 6

3. Vanaspati Ltd. consigned 5000 kg of Vanaspati Ghee to Ashoka Dealers, Chandigarh. Each kg of ghee costs ` 80. Vanaspati Ltd. paid ` 500 for carriage, ` 2,500 for packing and ` 2,000 for insurance in transit. After 3 months from the date of consignment of goods, Ashoka Dealers reported that 3500 kg of ghee was sold @ ` 95. per kg and expenses were ` 5,000 on godown rent and ` 7,500 on salesman salary. Ashoka Dealers are entitled to a commission of 5 per cent on sales. 500 kg of ghee was accidently destroyed in the godown. Insurance claim of ` 35,000 was admitted. Prepare the necessary ledger accounts in the books of both parties. 12

4. (a) Explain briefly how debtors ledger is made self-balancing. How do you deal with a transfer entry from one personal ledger to another ? 6

(b) What is a Single Entry System ? Distinguish it from Double Entry System. 6

5. (a) Explain the meaning and accounting treatment of the terms 'Life Membership Fees' and 'Tournament Fund' while preparing the final accounts of non-trading concern. 4

(b) Shiv Shankar & Sons purchased a car for ` 50,00,000 on April 1, 2013. The car was depreciated at 10 per cent under the written down value method. On April 1,2016, they changed the method of depreciation from written down value method to straight line method without changing the rate. Show the Car Account from April 1, 2013 to March 31, 2017. 8

6. Write short notes on any three of the following : 4×3=12

(a) Salient features of joint venture

(b) Materiality concept

(c) Ascertainment of credit sales in single entry system

(d) Reserve and Provision

(e) Rectification of one-sided errors

ECO-2

BACHELOR'S DEGREE PROGRAMME

Chapter 17: Term-End Examination, December, 2021
ELECIVE COURSE : COMMERCE

ECO-2 : ACCOUNTANCY - 1

Time : 2 Hours

Maximum Marks : 50

Weightage : 70%

Note : *Attempt any four questions including Question No. 1 which is compulsory*

---

1. From the following transactions, make accounting equation and prepare the Balance Sheet :

Transaction	Amount (Rs.)
(i) Mukesh started the business with cash	80,000
(ii) Purchased goods for cash	28,000
(iii) Purchased goods on credit	20,000
(iv) Purchased furniture for cash	6,000
(v) Paid rent	2,000
(vi) Received commission	500
(vii) Withdrew cash for personal use	3,000
(viii) Sold goods on credit (Cost Price < 30,000)	40,000
(ix) Paid to creditors	15,000

2. How is Bank Reconciliation Statement prepared from the adjusted balance of Cash Book ? Discuss with example. 12

3. Explain both the methods of determining profit under Single Entry System of Accounting. 6+6

4. On 1st January, 2020, 'X' of Delhi consigned to 'Y' of Mumbai goods for sale at invoice price. 'Y' is entitled to commission of 4% on invoice price and 20% of any price realized beyond invoice price. Goods costing < 12,000 were consigned to 'Y' at the invoice price of < 14,400. The expenses on sending the goods amounted to < 1,000. On 31st March, 2020 an account sale was received from 'Y' showing that he had sold goods worth < 12,000 in respect of 4 3th of the quantity of goods consigned to him. His actual expenses amounted to < 600. 'Y' accepted the bill drawn by 'X' for < 5,000 and remitted the balance due from him in cash. Prepare consignment account and 'Y' account in the books of 'X'. 12

5. Give the journal entries to rectify the following errors :
12

(i) A sum of < 600 written off as depreciation on Machine was not posted to Depreciation A/c.

(ii) Purchase Returns Book was overcast by < 300.

(iii) < 880 stolen by ex-employee stood debited to Suspense A/c.

(iv) < 1,000 received from a customer as advance was credited to Sales A/c.

(v) Purchase of a Scooter was debited to Conveyance A/c < 6,000. Firm charges depreciation @ 10% on vehicles.

(vi) Payment of < 300 to Ramesh and < 400 to Rajesh was made but Ramesh was debited with < 400 and
Rajesh with < 300.

6. Explain different types of Reserves. Distinguish between 'Provisions' and 'Reserves'.
6+6

© Author and Publisher 2024

9 789369 726752

Printed at Repro India Ltd.